AT MY EASE

AT MY EASE:

Uncollected Poems
of the Fifties and Sixties

by

David Ignatow

■

Edited by Virginia R. Terris

BOA Editions, Ltd. ■ Rochester, NY ■ 1998

LC #: 97–72087
ISBN: 1–880238–55–1 paper

First Edition
98 99 00 01 7 6 5 4 3 2 1

Publication of this book was made possible in part
by a generous donation from Chelsea Associates, Inc.
BOA Editions, Ltd.—a not-for-profit corporation
under section 501 (c) (3) of the United States Internal Revenue Code—
is supported by grants from the Literature Program
of the New York State Council on the Arts,
the Literature Program of the National Endowment for the Arts,
the Lannan Foundation, the Sonia Raiziss Giop Charitable Foundation,
the Eric Mathieu King Fund of The Academy of American Poets,
as well as from the Mary S. Mulligan Charitable Trust,
the County of Monroe, NY,
and from many individual supporters.

Cover Design: Daphne Poulin-Stofer
Cover Art: "White Shadow," photograph by Patricia Wilder,
courtesy of the artist
Author Photos: Christopher Conforti
Typesetting: Richard Foerster
Printed in the United States by McNaughton & Gunn
BOA Logo: Mirko

Most of the poems in this book were previously compiled (in somewhat
different arrangement and without the editing herein) on the worldwide web
site of John Fowler, GRIST-On-Line, under the titles *Gleanings: The Uncol-
lected Poems of the Fifties* and *Gleanings II: Uncollected Poems of the Sixties*.
BOA Editions, Ltd., gratefully acknowledges permission to reprint.

Other acknowledgments may be found on pages 128–129.

BOA Editions, Ltd.
Alexandra Northrop, Chair
A. Poulin, Jr., President & Founder (1976–1996)
260 East Avenue
Rochester, NY 14604

CONTENTS

THE SIXTIES

for Virginia

PREFACE

In the fifties, I became aware of my style of writing. It was inextricably bound with my life as a New Yorker. There were the subway, the crowds, as now, and the workplace, each in its electric atmosphere demanding speed and efficiency to be overcome if the individual were to survive. It was at the sacrifice of the emotional and imaginative self, as I experienced it. I brought it home from work, to the dismay of my family, recreating the tensions with which I had endured the day.

Love and intimacy were overshadowed. I saw it my necessity, my salvation as poet and as human being, to make such an existence the subject of my poems. The struggle was to find the style. It had to be won from the nature of the subject. It had to compensate the ugliness by being the aesthetic principle of ugliness itself in practice. It demanded receptivity to anger, sarcasm, satire, brutality, indifference and anguish, anguish with which all this was presented. Love and intimacy were without hope. In brief, it was the life of the New Yorker of my temperament and circumstance.

The poems in this collection were not given their final version in time for publication in *Poems: 1934-1969*. It's just as well. I offer them as the conclusion to a period of social and personal fragmentation. They were written with the same intention as those published in book form, that is, to make order and meaning out of unhappiness, an ironic task, but writing created distance between myself and my subject. The poetry stood apart from the thing itself. It was a reality of its own kind. From it, I could look out upon my immediate world with a lens of my own making and feel free, at least for the moment, and with a sense of mastery.

I wish for all my readers a similar experience of pleasure and relief as they read these poems.

David Ignatow
January 7, 1994

 # THE FIFTIES

 PART I

RESOLVED

Do you love?
Then you are wretched:
you have been hitched
to a plow, the ground
is hard and dry. It has
not rained for forty days
and nights. Now pull,
sweat and tears
will make the soil
fertile. Up will spring
the wheat of your bitter contribution.
Eat with horror
and increase of strength.
Pride returns
in the knowledge of your achievement.
It is possible to be happy.

■

STORY

A woman passes by an apartment house
with her husband. Upstairs a man
is walking around in his shorts.
The woman is engrossed in talking
to her husband. Upstairs
the partly-nude man wanders
from room to room.

■

LISTENING

It's to hear the children under my window
perform the ritual dance of sex to know
I am asking for an end to danger and death,
for the dance of shouts and gestures
is toward life, which is for danger and death:
a rush toward an ecstasy for destruction,
and I am with them: my heart beats
to the pounding of the feet, the pulsing voices.

■

PASSENGER

This one on the platform,
her smile twisted, the lipstick
distorted, in her black fur coat
and hat, is defiant, her smile sharpening
as the train approaches and vanishing
with the train's arrival.
She boards with an assault motion.

■

RUSH HOUR

That tall, shapely blond standing at her husband's side
on the station platform, as though he were her last defense
against her instincts, brushes up against him
and looks down at the newspaper he holds open
in front of him, and looks back at the crowd,
her lips firmly restrained. If I should meet her alone

one morning, as I already have, exchanging looks,
if we should meet once more,
we will not talk to one another.

■

PRINT SHOP

Here are the pin-ups of the nude,
nubile tits and shadowed bellies
lying in wait with bleak, amused smiles.
And these men at the type fount
find it inconvenient to look up
and wink or brush against them
to and from the composing table.

Off the rushed streets I come
with business figures crowding in my head
and stagger, silent, but catch myself
quickly. These men could think me
queer for looking.

■

OLD MAN

The girl who has been whistled at
by the fellows turns to me
with pleading eyes.

■

THE EXECUTIVE

The women who work for us—
we know this is how
they make their living,
not of love.
As men, we have declined
the role, and the women
at five walk out
into the evening.

■

Love is his nemesis: it follows him into sleep
to sit there playing its guitar, head
bowed above the strings. He listens
to the sound that could release him
into the music of the human condition:
love with its subtle anthem in his ear
to send him sailing to his brilliant home
of sun and sky, where he would sing
his way to joy in the body he has left
since he was born to live like every other
man and woman, at a job.

■

THAT I AM

Live because you have a sweet face.
You lean back slightly as if to take
comfort from your serenity. You are
so mild. Live though you are helpless
without me, unless in death I provide
for you. Let me go first. Your mildness

melts into the sun in whose heat
I am afraid I will lose you. Be well,
be firm if you must, be mild,
and save our lives to show the sun
and earth that we are a third
without which it is empty to discuss
between them.

Are you listening,
serenity I love? Does this voice
penetrate to you to pierce the sun
that shines and weakens you into immobility?
Your eyelids flicker, your smile appears
directed at me. Your sun now shines
on me.

■

Black eyes, snub nose, wide mouth,
its curves softly appealing—this
could have been you when we were young,
when, I remember, our lives together
were difficult and fine, in which
we grew old.

I looked back at this girl,
whose eyes continued to urge me,
as though in her impulse to give
I had not aged. I turned my head
away and looked out the window
of the speeding train, thinking.

■

INDIGNANT LOVER

To go panting after another male
who has to wear trousers, his legs hairy;
his genitals bounce without trousers to brace them,
he could be hurt, and each day must sit down
to stool and grunt or curse accordingly.
Is he thinking of love, with a job to get to
in twenty minutes and breakfast not yet eaten?
Is he harboring soft instincts
and the thought of giving—when giving
is what is wanted five days a week;
Saturday to get drunk on it
and Sunday church to ask forgiveness
and Monday to start again giving?
Is that one to run after? And am I
not like him whom she must chase and call,
My man? What am I then?

■

A SONG

For having loved my parents
I can swim the sea. I can breathe the air.
I can eat my bread. For having loved
their faces, I am alert to birds.
For having loved their sadness,
I am free, and for having loved their hands,
I am myself.

■

Something of ourselves, we decided finally,
to give our love content, not that we did not
know we had each other, but then

it did seem we could use as strength
the presence of another.

We would brood separately
and come together, even sulkily
so as not to lose heart for living,
and that was how we lived.

■

MARRIED

To Howard he said, "This morning I am tired."
If he could have told he had spent the night
thinking of the difference in the values
laid on money and love and yet money
without love was valueless, while love
could not exist without money to spark it;
if he could have said all these thoughts
kept him awake, Howard behind his desk,
littered with contracts, would have replied,
grinning, "Didn't you sleep at all?"

■

LOVE

Watching from across the table your shoulders
hunched to the food, your fork sliding
in and out, nothing could be more serious,
your face tense, removed, I think,
my glass idle in my palm, this is how,
by first strengthening ourselves,
we prepare a paradise.

■

ELIZABETH

Lying with my knees hugged to my breasts,
I would not care who came softly
to take away my ache.

■

SUBWAY

I am sorry, she would say:
That's all right, I would murmur.
She stood with her back toward me,
my nose nearly touching. The train
lurched to the right, giving me
the space to breathe in freely,
and I waited for the swing back
when I would have to lift her
from my chest, with my two hands—
how else?—braced against her buttocks,
and I waited
in the sober spirit of the ride.

■

SEPARATE WINDOWS

The young woman seated at her window
lost in thought and the young man
across the street—he has the urge
to stand naked at his window. He
steps back against a wall
and strips and returns crouching.
Slowly he begins the undulations
of love, stretching out his arms
to the air to embrace it, she
still seated but now noticing.

His movements increase in tempo,
he becomes taut, his motions compulsive
and spasmodic, trembling him. He sags,
hanging his arms,
and the young woman has risen to her feet
and stands still.

■

ADULTERY

The yellow kimono I gave her on the dark stairway
as a gift is worn now in the light of her bedroom
for her husband's eyes. He believes she bought it
to please him. It could very well be.
In loving me, she found the love for her husband
translated into a yellow kimono he could not afford.

I vanished from her sight long ago.
The dark, damp, dusty back stairs where we met,
I on my knees before her, she queenly supine,
still stands. Each morning on my way
to work I pass it—in the same building
where I earn my pay.

■

A summer of buttocks
tumescent ripe bellies
sweet legs
heads that nod
I am watching
not unhappily.
My life dreams itself
away.

■

OBSERVED

Reality is the other person.
We are all imagination
on whom the other intrudes
to give us pain and sorrow
from our unfulfillment
in the other.

■

It fills me to love you,
your face a creation of mine.
I create your love for me.

■

Success in the touches of your hand
upon the house. I see it clean
in unsuspecting corners. You were there
by instinct, my eyes searching
to understand.

Fame in your happiness at my labors
I bring from field of steel.
My eyes bleed but heal in your sight.
Art in our singleness
like garments clinging
in the wind.

■

 PART II

AMERICA

Our lives are broken up like bread
to be swallowed at breakfast,
feasted on at lunch
and downed for dinner.

At night we sleep
for the miracle of waking
whole again and free
and like the sun
find ourselves
on the same path
towards dismemberment.

■

NEW YEAR'S EVE

I sit here glad, glad of my comfort and so somber
that there is a wind for which I have no wise words.
And as it has no thoughts of its own
neither have the trees nor the people.
There are no wisecracks for such kinds of thoughtlessness.
And so I am fond of the wind as of any thoughtless
person, safe from either, with nothing to say
to one or the other, as I would have nothing to say
to throngs on 42nd Street, streaming in and out
of subways and theaters, they neither able
to make great decisions in their person
nor to act decisively on the world,
and so, between these two conflicting and frustrated
needs, decide finally to end up as theatergoers.
I, seated in comfort at home, still hearing
the wind, make no allusion to criticism,
knowing what the wind means for us all.
We will be blown out of this world,

with talk on our lips. We will be blown away
and we will have others in our place
who will try just as hard to make sense,
to talk straight and bitter, sarcastic
and penetrating and end up tossed like leaves
upon the ocean of wind and carried seaward
with the helplessness of the newborn.

■

You spouting about money
and I soaked through
standing in front of you
transfixed, believing money to come
pouring from your mouth,
I see so little of it.
Pour to me of the pleasures
of being poor: the hard bread
problems we have managed,
set up markers for those to come by
after us who are advancing short, strained steps
beyond where those before us
turned aside to die.

■

THE CHILDREN

In the morning they ran, warm and dressed,
to climb the ice pack jammed from shore to shore
on the river at their door. Each took possession
of his "island" or "fort." Ice was everywhere
for their games. In this way the lunch hour
passed. The ice spread out with the widening river.
Its current flowed downstream,
and, when the children grew conscious

of the drift, they could no longer
touch hands from their floes.

They saw each other float apart,
and lying stretched out,
not to be swept off,
these islands their safety,
watched each other vanish
out to sea.

■

SUBURBIA

Have I died that I am alone so much,
my eyes fixed upon a wall? I wait.
Am I waiting in a cenotaph?
Here is a private cemetery, the cars
seem to say, speeding past,
and I am made to doubt myself,
for some bodies, though they move,
are dead, like cut snakes
that twitch into the night
and next morning.

The ceiling above makes me uncomfortable.
That I can see grass outside is heartening.
No dead thing may yet see, and so
I go forth to tread the grass
and to watch cars on their way
and to be seen walking.

■

TODAY

When my grandmother on my father's side
was dying, she lay on her back,
made rasping sounds. I was a child and I tiptoed
in and out of the room. Her children
and older grandchildren sat there
and waited. None of my uncles nor my older
cousins nor my parents spoke to me
and not to each other either,
not without whispering from their seats.
I went down into the street seeking
a familiar face that would address me
and to which at age four I could reply
in that same open and friendly way.
Today I bend over my wife's bed
to talk to her in low, gentle tones
to soothe her pregnancy and say gladly
that our newborn will turn our fear
into a living problem to cope with.

■

I WILL BE GONE

What am I if not a pattern of manhood?
What should I be if not a dimension of silence?
I have suffered my pattern, and the last of it
will be the beginning of life in the ground
of ants and grubs or in workings of the rain.
I will have become indifferent and detached,
without fear, no longer envious but happy
as a spark at night. I will be gone into the dark,
my real mother.

■

BEYOND THAT

I see a man and woman strolling together
down the street and suddenly ask myself,
Why are they here? Why walking the earth
as if in possession? And I am left
breathing quickly but then diverted
by a car in my path or a woman
whom I know or am attracted to.
Beyond that I will grow old.

■

SANDIS MOUNTAIN RANGE, NEW MEXICO

On the coarse brown hide of the mountain
over its rolling tongue of the road
we drive to the mouth of this carcass
piled above us, in its shadow.
Far into the vertebraed distance
the stubbled skin lies in plains.
Where we see water, it is an open eye
dead to the sun, and when we look up
the sun is its crawling maggot.

Only that a foot leans upon a pedal
sees us out of the cemetery of this body,
dead from before the time we were swamp.
Rubber, oil and steel die beneath us
for our deliverance, and where trees dress
the impoverished sky, our eyes open again
within our burying selves.

■

EPITAPH FOR A SOLDIER

Enderle, who died for his country,
lived on beans and corn and surplus vegetables
issued by Relief in the days of peace.
Then he was told to take a job,
any job, for rent, carfare and food—
if cooked at home. His clothes
would have remained his working clothes,
underwear changed not more than once a week.
Hard work would have been the job,
sweat in summer,
stink in winter.

■

The time comes when you are facing him
as by accident, as by sheer inadvertency.
You had been running from each other
in opposite directions, avoiding what
had to be done and now have run
the roundness of the globe to come
smack up against each other
from opposite directions.

There is no escape from growing up
and becoming a man, taking your father's
life—his fortune, his will, pride
and place—and setting him on one side
off the road he is blocking. He stays
where you have placed him, filled
with shame for himself and hatred
and a desire to die at once or to kill.
He dies slowly. You helped him to it,
and it will be so written and read
and remembered, with horror in it
because it is the one way that sends
a man to become religious and heartbroken

and fearful, filled with the mystery
of himself.

He turns to his own children
for justification, their need for bread,
clothes and shelter, and his pride
as a man capable of acting. The rest,
while waiting to act, is prayer,
and it is like the moment before going
into battle.

■

THE MEN

The deer shot, they walk up to it
as it lies there tossing its antlers,
and shoot again through the right eye.
First they had hit it in the haunches,
making it fall. It staggers up
on all fours, wobbling. The men
back away, astonished. The deer
charges head down at a tree
and butts its right eye against it.

■

BORN AGAIN

I meet you with a knife in your hand
and here am I holding a gun. We
listen to the gun go off and the knife
ping into the skin. Good-bye, but hello.
We are back in the cosmos together,
circling the sun and waiting
to be born again.

■

I play at death
to satisfy a curiosity
as to the reason
I cling to life.
It is when I feel death
closing about me
that I know I belong
to the breathing
and that I must preserve
this difference that consists
in knowing about death

■

FOR MY 41ST YEAR

The years are beginning to come
like strokes on the hour,
and I, hands clasped, waiting,
will have won time over to become
my friend, taking me in sympathy,
I giving myself to it
in trust.

■

IN REPLY

Yeah, it's important to live,
if you must know, but more
important is to live whether
in the end you do know.

Just breathe and you'll get the message.
Just eat or stand up and stab
the person across the table

with the bread knife. You'll know
and not be sorry because you'll know
and want to laugh how easy
you can turn the bread knife
on yourself.

■

A.G.

Quick, get him into his grave,
he was a gambler and a waster,
indifferent to pain in others,
forty years of it, his wife made ill
of it, his children blighted,
lives a jumble and a toss.
He lived to see one die of it.

Rich, brown loam wasted on his coffin.
What could grow from it?

■

The flower lover has picked a time bomb
out of the grass. People standing about
are too stunned to move
as it ticks.

■

THE QUESTION

It is bitter to have to stand at your parents' graves
and to hear psalms read in prayer by the rabbi.
All the years of their lives they would have nothing

37

to do with poets or poetry and now you stand
with the beaten and are one with them,
all that you have written suppressed in themselves
and ignored who live in fear of their lives.

For your parents there is no grief.
The good years with them were the early ones,
your childhood when you felt wanted.
It was when they started to make demands
of you that your love for them
came into question.

■

AND TO ME

I can see how a child
would believe it is new
to the world and needs
to be cared for
and I can see
how an old man near death
would require the same treatment
his death new to him
and to me.

■

He is organized to die.
Seeing the moment confront him,
he straightens up
out of his angers and puts himself
in its hands without another word,
at peace with it but not with himself
since he understands death to be final
while what he must do with himself

alive will never meet the standards
he has set, death only making him
perfect in himself.

■

 PART III

The pavement has its life
and the dust in the air has its life
but the pavement that lies flat
for my footsteps—that is its life,
as dust is for our oblivion.
It settles upon me at home
and in the street.
If I believe I am superior,
think of the dust that does not waver
from its object
nor the pavement
from its path.

■

THE SUN

After a long walk, a long nap,
a return in spirit to overhanging foliage
of the trees, their trunks at spaced intervals
like temple columns. Far off, between
these trunks the sun gleams
like armor under the sun.

How to stay here without having to leave
to eat or to work? What more can a person
want who is unhappy? Overhead, peace,
calm, cool silence, the sun arrogant
in the distance.

■

AUTOBIOGRAPHY

If he knew how scared I was of him,
he would not let my subdued voice

rule him. It is low out of consciousness
of my power, he thinks. We both are awed
but for different causes, and so the status quo
for which both of us are grateful.

If I detect his scorn
of my inferior physical condition,
which he could overcome in a moment,
I also may detect his bafflement
at the consequences he cannot imagine
without terror. He feels powers
beyond him that could crush him.
If I do not possess these powers,
I walk in their reflection.

■

THIS MYSTERY

Thinking keeps me from the fright of the outside,
and when the thought vanishes I become sleepy
or bored or tired and very vague. People withdraw,
puzzled, or are made hostile and perhaps disgusted.
I am secretly delighted but disturbed
that sensing I wish to escape they will close
the exits and force me to speak up
and act as they.

Without arousing suspicion, then,
I hurry as fast as I can to an exit,
the day's end leading to my cave
where I move with the speed of thought
and am weightless as in space
that I have made for myself, thinking.

I want to get away from life
that has no end and no beginning.
I do not want to listen to reason,

except my own in which nothing is known
but that I am where I wish to be,
buoyed up by its mystery.

■

SELF-ANALYSIS

I am not writing because I feel as though
I am standing in my grave, looking out
upon the poetic excitement among the poets,
the businessmen stashing it away,
the lovers exuberant, the executives fierce
in their vision of efficiency. Each
has life by the hair.

Yet each will stand dumb, the poetry of their lives
will have come to a standstill. It will not occur
to them that they have carried the burden
of their charge to its limits, the poem taking over
and writing itself on their faces
as puzzlement and anguish. The poem will have
        become
the ruler of their lives to shape them
as it seems fit, as objects in the universe
of charged particles. They will end their lives
standing in an open grave and looking about them
at the crowds poetically mad with themselves,
in actions fit to their desires and singing.
We will hear their singing of money, of power,
of love, of success, and we will see it wind down
to their puzzlement and frustration and disbelief,
victims of their dreams.

■

I WRITE

I write to live as my heart beats.
No one shall misconstrue it
as anything but my heart beating.

Sick, weary of life, afraid of what's to come,
tired of striving, ashamed of what I have missed,
I listen respectfully
and take from its rhythm the thought
to make nothing else matter
but the steady beating of my heart.

■

I am like a scrap of paper stuck
to a turning truck tire.
I have no idea where I am going,
my senses dizzied by the motor's roar.
I am drowning in gas fumes
and the time keeps crushing
me to myself.

■

DREAM

This life is a nightmare lit up
by the sun, the moon and guns
flashing. I crawl for a throat
or a purse, asleep,
hidden away in a dream
of peace and plenty,
and in the morning
am prepared to kill or rob.
Do I laugh now and talk

with my friends? We are
hostage to each other.

■

A rock is thrown at my head
and I say, Ah, this rock
pleases me. It comes from anywhere
and is a greeting, and made me welcome
in a way I understand.

It was my enemy.
Harm is its stock in trade.
Knowing what's in store for me,
freedom to be in heaven, as it were,
while here on earth to sing hosannas
that I will have died but once.

■

THE DIGGER

Where I thought I had struck a well,
digging deeper I came on stone
and deeper still I found myself
sweating and angry in the sun
beating upon me in a hole.
I looked up and saw the sun
light the way to the surface.

■

SIMPLY

I must set a shape in air
and so I have chosen
the form of man.
As I am alive
I must live for my senses
and so I have my own peculiarity.

I live with my hands upon others
whose movements give me the sense of life,
my feet upon the ground for my weight
and my eyes to find their likeness,
my mind to set a seal
upon these satisfactions:
neither lion, coyote or bug,
simply this man
that I am.

■

AFTER WRITING A POEM

I do not want to be seen or heard or spoken to.
In the house I am grateful if it is empty
except for me. Only with wincing do I emerge
from my room, even into my wife's presence.
I am clean of all desire and passion,
clamor has died out in me. I am still
and peaceful. I think I exist
not in myself but in the air, unseen,
as I feel, unliving. I should say,
like Merton, that I sense myself in God
and do not wish to come out to live again.

I have lived and died by my own hand
and to come back is to break this pact

with myself, once more the crime committed
and I again without faith. But in presence
of my sin I grow restless and once more turn back
to rhythms of silence and alone again
take up a pen with which to commit myself
for one hour to eternity.

■

TOMORROW

Tomorrow is my sin
when in the evening I will wonder
what is to be gained by another day
won from death. In the daytime
I will shout and pound with the rest
on the work tables and will have forgotten
in my excitement my incapacity, fully awake
to my deception.

For one who wishes to live
there must be forgiveness
if I may forgive myself
who cannot be whole entirely.

I have love of wholeness.
I have love. I have myself
capable of this knowledge.
I have a perfection,
if you could call it that,
something of wholeness
and I shall be forgiven
at least in part, that part
which is me shall forgive myself
for incapacity. That which is
others will forgive me
if it must forgive itself.

That much I will have won
from my sorrow.

■

THE SAINT

There is someone smiling at me from behind
and someone holding out a hand in front
to say hello and persons unfamiliar
with familiar ways on either side
to put me at my ease. I should despair.
I do despair.

Where are the stones strung around my neck
I much prefer to carry, on hands and knees
and friends to lift me by my shoulders
to take the necklace from my neck? They
do not understand that I, without it,
am just a person like themselves,
unhappy, going to the help of others,
in the illusion that it sets them free.

■

SUBWAY

As the train door opens I am hoping
that a man with a giraffe's head will walk in
and take his place in the aisle
with the passengers. I want
a giraffe's head looking down on me
in my seat as I ride to work.
I want to be scared, amazed,
shook up.

■

What has brought me to you, stone,
when nothing in you can express a thought
or emotion? On the surface you are
what you really are, hard without shape.
Still, when I look I think of weight,
of crushing power.
                           This dialogue
between us is onesided, of necessity.
I give you the power to suggest
to me my own thoughts, but I cannot
let it rest at this, that I make up
my world, of my own need.

■

Poets I have refused to read
remind me of my misery,
for there is nothing else
with which to address oneself
to the world that moves
like a cloud of elephants,
and every person's identity
is of his own stomping.

■

ABOVE AND WITHIN

In the distance a phalanx of black clouds
descending upon the spot I sit in and read.
Overhead the sky lit with the last rays
of the day. I look down on my book,
for a moment, it seems. When I look up
again, the phalanx has not moved,
but above me the sky has darkened,

of itself perhaps, with the earth's revolution
away from sun.

Where I had seen a semblance of light
now stands darkness, nearly as absolute
as in the distance, and it has come upon me,
as it were, from behind my back. I feel overtaken,
caught between two pitiless forces.
I have one recourse left:
to bow my head and let the night reign
above and within.

■

BESIDE THE SEA

From my car I felt I was a vessel
of the waters. I longed to be filled,
my belly upturned,
my head pillowed upon the tide:
dead and drowned. And I would reply,
but not without being present,
for I would not be lying still
upon its bosom were I not welcome.
And the car took me to my Sunday relatives.

■

BUSINESS

What are they trying to say
who neglect to pay me their bills,
and my own creditors hounding me?
I bent myself to their needs;
it was personal, apart from the money—
as if they would turn to me
in everything. Between us

we would live in ease. And now
I cannot get my money. I will call
and tell them the mistake is theirs
to have reduced me to a simple need
for money.

∎

OFFERING

My work has become the making of tragic poems
to denounce me for my failures, each one
telling me of my selfishness and ungenerosity
toward others, of my inability to unbend.
I remain still, humble and ashamed in myself
to have given my poems a share of my bitterness,
now turned against me. I turn to my wife
as she takes my hands, knowing how I suffer
for being damned with my own deeds
and she protests. Do I not realize
I have a tree to sit under
and the whispering of its leaves
to listen to? They play about my head
and at my feet and have a father
to acknowledge them.

∎

I leaned, ballooning my shirt,
delivered as space
in the clinging air,
in love with myself,
and in the shouting peace
of love I saw the sun's need
for the heavens. It was
when I returned to breathing
that I thought, Flesh contains me;

where then have I been
that I am so happy now?

■

So here are all of you
to hear me read
what I have written in private
to please myself. What if
the next line is about shit?
Because shit is always there.
And you have come to hear what I have to say.

Are you already leaving?
Well, I'll go with you.
It's not easy to write about shit
all by oneself, if you can't have
anyone to complain to.
Let's go to a restaurant
and load up and tomorrow you'll think
about me.

■

ON THE BOWERY

There are times I refuse to wash myself
as if I would have the dirt and sweat
of that day stay until tomorrow,
for each day goes by in dirt and sweat,
washed off each evening, with not much thought
of what it is I wash off, another day
of my life.

    I should pray with each washing,
for I am letting go down the drain
a part of me I must miss forever—

bit by bit until I wash my life away,
for all I really have to show is this
dirt and sweat I cling to as my only
evidence of having lived, my one
accomplishment and pride.

■

THE PEN

When I lay it down I'm bewildered,
without a country, and I walk about
in danger of being stopped
and questioned and looked at
straight through to my weakness,
just another person in the street
hoping not to be hurt in traffic
or mugged
or jailed
for wanting to live.

■

SLEEPLESS

At this moment two swans in Babylon
shake their feathers of the night
and nestle together among the water thickets,
no happier and no sadder for it either,
but wait as I wait
in this thicket of a room
for the first break in the dark.

■

If I can walk farther
than my pain can reach
I'll have entered
a new birth.

■

Waiting to live,
living to wait,
and we cannot explain it
nor get beyond it
nor find ourselves
in another phase—
but to hear our breathing,
see ourselves seated,
think of ourselves waiting.
It is possible we are waiting
to die. At this point,
we get up, annoyed, impatient,
to assert ourselves,
acting as we wait.

■

IN THE FIELD

for George Oppen

The bull lunges at you!
Run, do not look back,
your hands, your mind vacant
with fear!

You make a stand,
whirl, and with hands on hips
lean towards the bull's eyes.

The animal wavers, snorts
and slows to a trot,
shaking his horns from side to side.
Still at a distance,
he turns away
to nibble grass.

But mind moved by his jaws,
he charges blindly,
once more to feel your eyes,
and lowers his head to the grass
at your feet.

■

OVERHEAD

Overhead the elevated straddling the library
made a cool shade in summer. Across the street,
framed between two steel pillars, a dirt path
led through a grass lot to a hint of country life:
two-story wooden houses and chicken coops.

When, father-voiced, the rumbling train passed
above, the chickens cackled of their decisions
and appetites. For me, age twelve, there were
sounds of waterfall gods who lost themselves
in mist below as motion without matter,
effort without force, a heaven,
on every hand the signs and portents
of sublimity. I embraced its configurations
but in human role, with faculties of sight,
hearing and delight: my object pleasure
and my meaning self.

I awoke to the sound of my own steps.

■

FIRST GENERATION

He sang and jogged the paper sheets,
his belly against the work table,
the sheets leaning against his belly,
his broad chest lifted as he sang
lustily a lament from the old country
learned from his parents,
and as it ended with a flourish
he grinned broadly at those working
beside him jogging their sheets,
and, like him, American.

■

QUESTIONING

I am here.
Am I in the councils of the government?
I ask because I do not hear my name
spoken as I sit at my desk.
I do not hear myself being called
or discussed. Looking up
from my window, I think the
sky is as detached as I am
from my life
and perhaps for the same reason.

■

IN THE PARK

It was a day of feeling.
It was our world, the lake at our back,
in front of us the cars scooting past.
We were in no hurry where we sat.

It seemed right, with nothing to make us
leave or want to leave, but then
those cars reminded us of worlds
going in so many directions.

Without wanting to admit it,
this too had its beautiful side
because of being so futile,
this bother and rush people persisted in
as if nothing else existed;
that if this was what they persisted
in doing then it was possible nothing else
did exist.

■

THOUGHTS OF A TINY PIG

If I had a different life to live
this would be the foolish one—
to root, hog, sleep and procreate.
Always across my mud hole I see
the farmer waiting for my size
to grow, as he leans close up upon his rake.
I do not even want to be the farmer
nor the wife whose pig is well done,
but the stranger passing by
out of curiosity and anxious
to get away from the smell.

■

THAT I AM

Face to face with my stubborn self
that refuses to yield up to me

in verse the secret of my life
I am ready to transmute
into a poem, assured that it will live
as I now live, the poem to have
its stubborn quality of being:
harsh, ungainly, unhandsome
and unyielding, gripped by anxiety
for tragedy, the one truth
I can depend on to endure,
but it is that which refuses to yield itself
to my desire to change into a poem
and is the poem in its absence.

FOR WALT WHITMAN

I cannot read you
without feeling my life
betrays you. I set you
aside with disdain
for you make a big thing
of existence when I know
it is simply the dropping
of a token into the slot
and of riding downtown
in the subway.

How would you like
to be pushed out
by your camerados
all getting off with you
at your stop and rushing
to have their coffee
first before facing
the boss?

MEMOIR

It was that time when I could sit by a window
and read books. Naturally, I grew fat,
and the books heavy. Blooming out from behind
in tight knickers, I cruised between library
and window chair, airily like a yacht.
On the street I heard cursing by foreign kids
not in found books.

Right through me the kids shouted.
I could have been air, as I crossed
their games, hurt at being invisible.
In the library, the books smelled of leather
and paper dust. I would pull back my head
out of the press made by the leaves
and thought the smell not unpleasant
but close, binding me in. I needed air.
Out in the street, one arm hooked
around a pile of books, I walked,
feeling the crippled position of my arm.

MY STORY

I accept the candle handed to me
out of the dark where I hear
the thunder of Roman troops.
The candle is lit, floating down
from over the heads of the fighters
against Rome. I place it
in a candle holder and set the light
beside my bed. In its ray
the thunderous troops recede.
I pick up a history of the Jews
and read. My story.

■ PART IV

DEAR SIR

So you're out of work,
don't have money,
need food in the house
and have written a letter to the
President, Dear Sir:
I voted for you in the last election,
expecting you to curb the Reds,
put down the campus rebellion
and lead the people back to peace.
So far, I find my neighbor and I
are out of jobs and hurting.
But is this to say
that you have to start with us first,
working backwards, eh?

■

CAREERS

The printing press thunders out
advertisements for brassieres
and girdles in four colors. Do you
have any idea of the time, effort
and skill that have gone
into building this machine?
Careers are built on it,
marriages made
and families founded.

■

STAYING RELAXED

Man, see the trucks going by loaded
with goods! Who will unload them?
And hear the roar of their motors.
Powerful, eh? And you seated
on a fire hydrant. Speak up.
People are waiting to be fed,
clothed, housed, entertained
and doctored. Speak, man.
What are you doing, then,
seated on a fire hydrant?

I'm doing all right.

■

Who are these men who become plumbers
and work at it diligently
in the toilet, the basement, the kitchen,
skilled at their vocation and proud
of their ability, wherever they appear,
with tool chests slung from their right shoulders
in cold water or on their backs, staring up
at the elbow of the kitchen drain
and determining the cause of the stoppage.

I am in their world,
pen in hand, wishing them well and celebrating
their pride, earning their wages
at needed work.

I watch each detailed movement
of arms and fingers, as if they held
the answer to my problems. They go about their work
with so much assurance that I think
they already understand everything

else that's wrong, and if I but study
their movements I will learn
how to repair what's broken in me.

■

THE DAGUERREOTYPE

Your father at twenty, mustachios,
high-buttoned shoes, tight suit,
stands one foot forward, cane planted
in front of him, hand gripping it
firmly: "I know my cane and I know
at what I'm looking, being photographed;
my passport to the world I stand in fear of,
except I have my bold style.

You ran errands for him,
delivering meat, chickens, eggs
in the snow before school time.
In the dark before going to bed
you make the rounds again, taking orders
for the morning. A bird lying in the gutter
you stuff into your pocket, hoping
to revive it with your warmth,
later to bury it in a hole you dug
for it, brushing dirt back in
to cover the body. You will not defy
the world, nor make a showcase of it
for your pride. Your father works
a butcher shop and your mother too
waits on customers and grows angry
and tired and ill of the damp floor.
Your father, neat and small, staggers out
of the icebox, a whole side of beef
on his shoulder.

■

SUMMARY

In life we solve no problems,
just bend them like crowbars.
A person takes one up
where we laid it aside
and advances upon us.

■

THEY SAID

They said your footprints were stamped in blood
all the way to Emergency, the blood flowing
down your face and onto your shoes
receiving the steady trickle.
Did you welch on a bet
or take another man's girl?
I do know I'm sick about it,
you resigned, moaning on a stool
in the white, immaculate room,
getting your lips and cheeks stitched.

Cops standing by get no answer
to their questions and would arrest you
to compound the folly. Perhaps
it would be best to lock you up
until you talk. You must be sick yourself
inside, your good looks gone, lips scarred
and swollen for always, for nothing:
money or drink or sex. You've got to wear the wounds
and feel hatred for the very things
that used to give you pleasure.

Say this and the cops will understand.
Say nothing and the sickness grows in everyone.

Say something, accuse no one.
Say what hurts.

■

NEW MEXICO

The sun blazes in silence
for there is no one to speak to
like the sun. The men sit
under it, bored, filled
with inferiorities and resentments
which they turn toward the blue onyx
of the sky, sending up planes
in defiance, whipping the air,
but nothing is said, for the sun
leaves behind its own contempt:
darkness and cold.

■

THE PROMISE

We sat upon splintered dock piles,
watching waves beneath run clear across
the river to the shore opposite,
as far off as the faint echoing tug boat
horn. A light beginning to show on portside
gleamed no bigger than a child's eager eye.
Farther out, tall buildings, hazed by sunset,
stuck up like thumbs from the swell
of the river, pregnant toward the brightening moon.

This was not heaven, we were forced to tell ourselves,
so close to the water's depth—the salt air
reminding us of the sea in the very throat

of the river, past the bay. But here the toot-toot
of tug boats wearing their jewelry of lights,
the chandelier of the sky suffused in its own glow,
we could believe the river, dark in the hollows,
streaked upon its crest with shine, was the ballroom
floor of the dance of the tidal veil trailing
the boats, the gulls winging applause: a dance
of the marriage of differences.

■

Man cannot leap over himself.
He must take himself with him
on the steep path to change,
if better is what he is seeking
in himself. I doubt it,
but I'm willing to suspend my disbelief
until tomorrow.

■

A RHYME

Do you know—I don't—what the trouble is?
It starts somewhere at the bottom
and works its way to the top.
It spreads around in a circle
until it comes to a stop,
and then it bores through the surface
and digs straight down through the ground
and what has been left standing
topples without a sound.

Do you know—I don't—what the trouble is?
For nothing is left of the matter
and no one can find out the cause.

It makes for some very sad chatter
and a very long pause.

■

SUMMER

Men and women at the beach
exhibiting themselves in briefs,
hoping to be touched, talked to,
embraced—the sea,
eye of the earth, observing them
and sending little messages
to return and be at
rest.

■

DIGNITY

Rocks jut out of the sea
and ships maneuver
to avoid them. One
sails steadfastly through,
fighting off an undertow,
and the rocks have dignity
they lacked before.

■

A SUMMING UP

Perhaps a table set for two, or a garden
at the end of day, but no more.
Mostly a walk through vacant spaces

in which sound assails us, and shapes
that are not visible oppress us with their weight.
We feel them about our faces, arms and shoulders
but see nothing and nobody, concentrated
on one thing—to eliminate or at least prepare
for those sounds.

If we are able by a sudden turn down one street
to block off those noises and those weights
upon us, we may find ourselves in a small room
fit for two persons, with a table between,
where they may eat or listen in silence
to one another's complaint of the outside—
and a garden that we had no idea could exist
in the rear. As we enter, its odor assails us
and since we are then out in the open
these sounds again and a noise of the invisible
shapes colliding among themselves.
Are the voices of these shapes in conflict?
We sit there but we cannot communicate their beings,
the noises in us, it seems, and the shapes
we cannot see making our bodies their weight,
they have become so familiar to us.

∎

ARMOR

How do I explain myself to a man
who thinks eating is pure pleasure?
He looks on the passing scene as he chews.
So that we can communicate, I speak
about his food being nicely seasoned.
He can smile at me between gulps,
talking about the passing crowds
of excited weepers and mourners
headed—where to?—in such numbers.

He would like to know to what disaster
or to whose funeral.

■

AS THEY FLY

Birds call out as they fly
to keep track of one another.
Each being one, all together
they let each other know
so that none forgets itself
and is lost.

■

DEAR HOMER

At five this morning I opened half an eye
and saw your rosy-fingered dawn
but I remembered it was simply time
to get up and put in some overtime
at the shop. In the kitchen would be
just my wife waiting for me to get out
so that she could get back in bed.
Baby keeps her up all night.

None of your people would be around, Homer,
but I had the thrill of thinking
how it was the same dawn as yours,
five thousand years between us.
I was a bit worried about that sameness,
though, thinking I had slipped back
to be with you and had lost my wife and baby,
some unconscious wish granted, perhaps,
but then I challenged myself to see chariots

and armed Ulysses and, naturally, none of his men
nor did Achilles step forward to say hello,
and that was what stood between us, Homer,
but I am writing so that you see I do believe
you're still around, as rosy-fingered dawn
keeps coming up.

■

At night the darkened windows
are like gaping holes in the flesh,
the battle lost.

Morning will come, brightening
the windows, we to look out
on the world and cheer
at its brightness.

■

CREDO

I say let us abolish the calendar,
let us live in a parabola,
not as though we were walking
from one shut room to the next
with the door slamming behind
to startle and frighten,
to make us hesitate.

Let us live with the seasons,
the way rains come in the autumn
and the sky changes to foreboding,
prompting us to vigorous response,
and the way winter approaches
in perceptible cold. We return

to our homes to sit out the cold
by the fire or, on the way out,
bundle up.

Spring arrives, a wing flashing
past the window, the snow still
on the ground and the rain now
but rain smelling of growth
and restlessness, for we are
looking toward flowers.
What harm then in this life
or death it asks of us,
with the seasons?

■

■ THE SIXTIES ■

 PART I

JOBS

Murder is one and loving is another,
not thinking, passing just to know
at the end of day that we are still breathing
and can get a smile out of the elevator man,
testing our wit on his passivity.

He takes us down from the hard acts
we have performed. He carries us back
to the ground, where we have something
to step on that does not complain.

We are leaving behind the dead
and heading for new beginnings,
for old endings. The victim is known.

Here I am and there you look at me
as if I had been the one to kill you
and I have not yet told you what
I think. It's when the dead
come to life again that I leave.
I dread returning.

■

You feed me and I give you iron and anger,
world of the narrowing air,
world without horror,
in sublime calm
in whose depths are no monsters,
merely stones.

Whom shall we fight
and for what reason is anger?
World of the sun shining on the hill
awakening from night to death,

brightly lit, my world.
Do not forsake me,
for I would forsake you first
for meaning,
for what leaving would mean
of horror and anger.

■

DIVORCE

You come, arms filled with packages and flowers
and look for me to smile a welcome. You are stout,
short, have just been divorced. Your jaw is heavy
and hairy, your nose long and rugged like a man's,
and when you speak everything else is made
even more queer by your squeaky voice.

I have been waiting for you to take my place
in the office, late, as I had feared,
despite my warning you and after having done you
favors to induce you to arrive on time
for once. At five after—I had lifted the phone
to notify our boss that I was leaving—
you arrived. I put down the receiver silently,
without smiling, angry at the waste emotion,
as if you had planned it this way
time after time to bring me to a boil
and you then step in smiling.

I have wanted to finish you off
by reporting your habitual lateness
and have you fired, only to find myself
frustrated by your silent appeal.
It probably took your husband many years.

■

I am indifferent to the girl standing
before me, her heavy belly over her knees.
I have her sit down while I type
and ask pertinent questions. Born where?
Birth date? Married? Yes, husband dead.
Standard formula for unmarried girls.
Another sits by, impassive, also unmarried,
husband dead. Registered last year
at the clinic on her own.

I hear the young hoods outside
the office window roaring their cars.
Impassive child,
after dark you creep out of the house,
your mother pretending not to hear
and let the boys take you
in dark halls to cover your loneliness.

You are going to find yourself
in a one-room apartment, with no heat,
and no facilities for washing the child.
No wash basin, no bathtub, no clean sink.
Just a window overlooking a brick wall
and children outside fighting, screaming.

■

SUMMERTIME

I'm thinking of a stout, sweating woman
seated in the train, a lollipop
stuck in her mouth. Passenger
across the aisle are staring.
She stares back, rolling the lollipop
from cheek to cheek.

Her blouse is unbuttoned
down the front, her fat knees

are uncovered. She has folded
her bare arms across her big breasts.
Passengers look away
as she sprawls in her seat,
sucking.

■

MOBILES

The artist Jones is seen standing in line
waiting to pay admission to a movie
in which adolescents undress each other
and perform sex. Jones then
drives back to his studio and examines
a new sculpture he has completed,
dislikes it
and turns it to the wall.
From now on he is going to work
only in mobiles.

■

Why is it that lying in bed
you scold me,
while up and about
making coffee you are interesting
to talk to, discussing art
or the dream? Why is it,
when my hand wishes
to consummate our interest
in each other by touch,
I hear a tiger
rising from your throat?
I see your toes curl like claws

while art and the dream
keep to their hovel.

■

I used to be in love
and don't know now
for what
as I struggle along
with the idea still imbedded
in my brain like a sore.

I used to be proud of my love.
It focused on pleasure
as against duty.
How is it that without so much
as asking permission they have
changed places?

■

LIFE AND ME

I'm only a bystander,
I once inhabited you.
Now you are about to leave,
first having made me weak
and ill, so as to force me
to want to be rid of you.

Well, we were once good lovers
and took care of one another.

I gave you ecstasy,
you returned it doubly.

All right, you are tired,
I too am tired because of you.
Let's call it a day.
It was good knowing you.
Remember me in your grave,
I will remember you
in these lines.

■

Before I met you I wasn't always sad.
I had friends.
You were an idea
I would contemplate in private
and when you showed up
I fell into an ecstasy and slumped
into despair. There was no way
I could discover that would keep you,
and yet you were there,
in my arms, in my thoughts.

I ate your voice, your touch,
your smile. I ate a dream,
I became a dream to myself.
Now I appeal to you
to be yourself, for my sake
that I may find myself.

■

I sit at my desk, listening to the phone ring.
If I don't answer it will fall silent
and I will have to think about,
worried at such silence in my life.
It will be quiet in the grave.

Reluctantly, I pick up the receiver
and hear, "I was about to hang up,
thinking you were gone," and
to shake myself of its meaning to me
I reply, "I would have called you."

■

It is peculiar that you should love me:
I see myself as a frog or toad.
Calmly I turn away.

There you go, pleading with me,
your voice strained and hoarse,
angry. Are you frog or toad too,
my arm laid across your shoulder?

■

What shall he do with a son
who believes he is being poisoned
by his parents to get rid of him?
Think of him as ill,
and human.

■

I hear my mother call me in my sleep
and I answer, Here I am, awake,
but remembering I am middle-aged,
with children in the room next door
whose care and feeding are my job.

I slide beneath the blankets to weep
in my heart for the mother of my safe childhood.
She fed me without qualms,

and there was my father each evening
in his chair reading the paper,
unperturbed by my presence.

What I have gained from my parents
I have to give to my children
with their milk.

■

I couldn't have loved you as a child.
You came a stranger.
I was a stranger.
We met on a lonely road.
Convulsed with trouble, you touched me,
troubled myself. I read identity.

Back to back we walked apart.
I love you as that part of me
that will not heal, and I love you
as through a glass wall
because writing I think I am well.

■

I whistled Brahms to tell you I loved you
and wanted you as my wife
to face with me perplexities. Brahms soft
and appealing at his lullaby best
to soothe and make you understand
without my speaking in the voice learned
from the streets of gangs.

You too were afraid
but for another reason
and over and over I whistled the melody,
the little that I knew of it

and none of its development,
until dry-mouthed I screeched
as I whistled, my throat strained,
and your hand came to rest in mine.

■

 PART II

The moment which is like a pear,
perhaps a touch of a hand,
a wanted kiss given,
a bought gleaming razor blade,
something to admire,
so bright, so dangerous.

I expect no answer other
than the moment that is aroused
in me and loved—my life.

I'll have moments stretching
like a string of pearls
into the distance, with death
no larger, no darker,
no less desired.

■

When I see life in short, deathlike scenes
between people, where each gives the other
the coup de grace, where then will I find
the great forms? Who will sit thinking
when his own door is expectant?

May death be swayed by our obedience:
we'll kill each other with a look,
each look warning first
with an averted eye,
death to know we are aware.

■

I live because death is the goal
and it is my intention to meet it
with a grace I have not been able
to bring to bear effectively

upon my life. With death, since
it will come of me, I can prevail
to win it over to a gracious end.

■

I am soon gone
to follow my father.
I belong next to him,
on the other side
of my mother, or
perhaps behind him
out of respect for privacy.

For him, he ended tragically,
not knowing whether I lived
or died before him
or whether I abandoned
him in his illness.

I leave this for everyone
to read that he was my father.
I did what I was taught by him,
to stay with truth
and never to leave it
for the sake of sentiment
and in deeper loyalty to him
it is to let him know
both of us had been betrayed
by a stranger hostile to us
whom he had warned against,
and I was telling him
in my absence from him
that he was right
and I was wrong
in trusting a stranger.

I kept faith
in the only way left to me
by my absence
from the house of strangers
in which he died.

■

People don't matter any longer.
It is the fact of death that matters
to all of us and it hurts,
as people once did but no longer,
now that I know they are with me
in the catastrophe of life,
over which we have no control,
and so are its parts within it
to act out the roles given each of us
to carry out the mandate of living.

We are its function of being and becoming,
as are the bees in their labor to perform
as bees, who know nothing of themselves
than what they are to do,
that is for us the step
that lets us move toward recognition
of ourselves for what we are:
to suffer it and accede to it
and affirm it with a helplessness
to do otherwise than that
which is suspect to us of being,
but another function yet of being,
and so to glory in our knowledge,
in flattery of our consciousness,
in pleasure with our bravery,
in sadness with the day to come.

■

The child had lost a friendly dog in an accident
and to be reminded of it made her shiver,
her head lowered toward her hands
which turned a small doll over and over.
It was being impressed upon her
that nothing lasted, while duties were
with her always, such as minding parents
and eating well and that we ourselves
were just as liable to disappear.
Did we not also love ourselves?
That meant we were just as vulnerable
as dogs and toys. The one she held
in her hand she turned over and over
unsmiling, as if looking for its wound.

■

TESTAMENT

I watched a tigress eat the deer
and I watched the deer lie still
being eaten and knew there was a connection.

I could look around for who or what
would be nourished by me. I saw first
that it was the earth to feed the roots
of trees and flowers. I could take my death
factually, with the calm of a foregone
event in my life.

And I did but loved to write about it
for the pleasure it gave
to make it live for me in my imagination
and then on paper for you to read.
It was a pleasure afforded by life.
I took it in great whole. I lived
and affirmed my living by writing

about it for others like myself
to read and know there is this joy
to living in the midst of death.

■

The night is calm
but for a truck
passing by and a boy's voice
with companions, free of their parents.
The truck is gone,
the voices drop into silence
and I am alone
with my awareness and breathing.

I am passing the time of my dying
like a voice or shifting of gears
about to pass into silence.

I lean back and think of Bill,
his books left behind,
an aged wife upright, calm
as the night, cheerful
as a boy's voice,
Williams, the voice of the maker,
silenced.

■

FOR WCW

We sat in rows listening to your poems
being read at your funeral. I heard them
as you would have read them. He's not
dead, he could never die, I said to myself.
This stuff's not for funerals,

whoever you are, reading from the pulpit
in a priest's garb. You are dead wrong,
the man still is with us,
bleating his lines.

■

"No ideas but in things"
and things die, leaving the words,
rhythms and sounds of what once was:
an echo, pleasant, devoid
of the strain of writing:
the voice of a bird echoing
in the silence: the beautiful past,
and sounds of the future,
as though one approaches a waterfall,
a murmurous roar, our nerves alerted
to beauty, to what is and is not,
and then over the falls into spray
and collisions, beauty absenting itself,
hiding in the spray
and in collision with water,
then death by drowning,
where beauty is gone
to where is death,
beauty in death,
in detachment from tumult
and spray: an echo,
a severed past,
a dismembered part.

■

THE STARS

Why do they shine so brightly if not to be themselves
completely? So it should be for ourselves,
unless like a dying star that bursts apart,
dwindles into space, the wars and diseases
are the symptoms of our coming end.

What does it matter, after all—
as another piece of the cosmos
turns into heaps of gas clouds
from which to start anew?

What does it matter that we are diseased with dying
and violence, as the signs that we are dying
are changed and change itself is life?

Praise the lord who is man,
praise the body and soul of man
who is his own creator, and praise
that of which he makes himself,
the first existence before his own.

This is the mystery, that it exists,
that it should be there
to make of it ourselves.

Such mystery is my religion,
and I am afraid I must die as gods die,
to be other than I know myself now
because it is in me to change.

■

THE JOBHOLDER

I stand in the rain waiting for my bus
and in the bus I wait for my stop.
I get let off and go to work
where I wait for the day to end
and then go home, waiting for the bus,
of course, and my stop.

And at home I read and wait
for my hour to go to bed
and I wait for the day I can retire
and wait for my turn to die.

■

 PART III

AGING

I see time as the time of the body.
So now that I see myself as time
I am about to move into the shadow,
out of the high sun, the shadow
that is cooling to my skin and brain.

I may do exactly what I had been doing
under the sun, but now I may do it
mildly, letting the heat mount
at my own pace, at my own degree
of warmth of skin and brain.
I become my own master
in the shade.

■

My eyes are forming a tree,
a net to catch the sun.
The branches are still,
the sun slowly fading
from their grasp.
I reach out,
fingers spread apart.

■

I look out on an empty road and I'm delighted
that I can travel on it in peace and silence
having to contend only with myself. A vacant, silent
road on which to dance freely,
lonely no more, resolved that loneliness
is a compulsion toward others.

I am seated by the roadside,
expecting someone to come by;
it seems so unlikely that this road can remain
vacant, there are so many others like myself,
perhaps seated by the roadside too
but expecting me which would make them weep
and grow sad, this road, its emptiness,
the possibility of death that is my love
for it, an emptiness that gives me to think
I am already dead, so peaceful and alone.

I will sit here at its wayside, road vacant
of purposeful beings, alone, silent,
without intent of its own, its construction
something else, for is it not to demonstrate
the virtue of silence and not of need
that makes it a pleasure to walk in?

■

My self is a watcher
and I sing now.
My self has a world
I call Being alone.

■

After the subway ride,
after the long walk from the station
and after the wash-up and sitting
down to dinner, after the brief sign
of affection for your wife and child:
a kiss, a nod, a pat, a glance
at the walls, familiar still
after listening to the news
and scanning the paper
for what you omitted reading

on the train, and after stretching
at the table and yawning,
you get up on your feet
and look toward your room that you may
or may not shut, in which you find yourself
singular and alone.
No child to run in, no wife to knock
politely that the phone or the doorbell—
for a moment and ask, What was it
that you thought was in you apart
from all this? And lie down thinking.

■

A vision of black rock—
I'm content to be as somnolent,
knowing its limitation,
this minimal ache.

The cardinal on the phone wire
has flown, taking its red brilliance:
a contrast to enjoy, as if
to look out of darkness is to spy
a meaning other than my own.

■

I fix my eyes on a blade of grass,
my heart beating nervously. The lawn mower
roars in the garden. The one blade
of grass I have chosen for myself,
sorting it out from its cluster,
is no different from others. I have had
to count from the right side
to arrive at the exact leaf on which
to fix my gaze.

I wait in a near sweat. I know the gardener,
clean-shaven, face round and full,
hands large, a broadchested salesman
on weekdays—good-natured, talkative,
energetic.

The lawn mower roars in circles,
fading and returning. The odor of cut grass
is keen, delectable. I wonder at myself
able to enjoy the smell, my eyes lowered,
my heart tight for that one blade of grass.

The mower grows steadily louder
and I more and more panicky. The roar is upon me.
It passes. He says hello, a questioning
look, as he grips the handle of his machine.
My eyes are still lowered, but now blurred,
my cluster scattered every which way.
I turn my head from side to side
to look without hope.
Calm, sad, resigned.

■

When I look at the faces that confront me
in the morning subway ride, I see the same
hopelessness and impassivity as mine
between the dark green walls of the train,
dimly lit overhead. We are riding
to the hopeless cause of making a living
just enough for a day.

The knife is in me.
No matter how I twist and turn,
it sticks, making the wound large.

■

THE STREET

So lonely, to wade in air
against a soundless wave
of bobbing heads. I believe
it is possible no person
in me exists, driven
to look outwards
for rescue.

■

In my dark mood I look out upon the street.
Back and forth the cars go, their colors bright.
It is strange that I cannot have
their bright look, when it is I
and persons like myself who ordered them,
to buy with an unhappy mind.

I look at trees and houses and it is a puzzle
that I can't have them inside me too,
in place of my unhappiness, where my desire
for them begins.

Why can't I have these cars, houses
and trees offering comfort to the eye
inside me? Why can't my thoughts
be bright as two-toned cars
and like a large house shaded
by tall trees?

Why can't they become my mind?
The dark thoughts stand outside me
like the truants they are, waiting
to be forgiven. Why is it they possess me
while I possess cars, trees and houses?

■

I am alone, mother, without you.
It's as if I have been deeply wounded
on the battlefield, with no one near
to help me to safety. I am alone,
as I was at your oxygen tent,
without you to turn to for a home.

Tomorrow I move out into the strangeness,
searching for you in the faces
of other women.

No tears, there is no life in tears:
this truth to clear my eyes
to give me direction.

■

I'd rather look around me
than within. I'd rather
admire the bedspread
and curtains to testify
to their presence: I
cover my sadness at being
alone.

■

Suffering is what I do best.
I do it so well, I am ashamed,
accepting it with my food.

Deprived of suffering,
how would I know myself?
The features that remain
after the burning out
I hold to as myself.

■

Exult among sad, resigned men
in their corners. Exult
as hordes advance like lava
across the burning plains.
I am aroused to contain them
or escape into a dream
of trees.

■

I come to joy when suffering begins
to turn on itself and its maker.
It is when I grow absolutely still
and sick that I begin to feel
the pulse of joy.

I know that if I would have
the whole of life in my history,
I must go through the narrow door
of suffering.

■

PORCH

I will sit out there and talk
about houses, taxes and land values
and which trains are best to catch
in the morning commute: all
that has sifted down from the great froth
of love and ideals.

The chair where I have sat listening
is worn round, my throat prepared
by a small niche from which that kind
of talk, like a needle placed to it,
begins to flow, like mucus.

But here alone, refusing for at least
one hour to be needled, I have this
satisfaction, this healing plaster
of a poem.

■

JOB HUNTING

Is it references you want?
Will Walt Whitman serve as my credential?
You'll find him in the library,
he'll be glad to talk,
and he will say what you will want
to hear.

We have known each other
almost from the start. We were
like one flesh, but that's for him
to tell you. What I need simply
is money for a doctor and Walt
is my reference, my only one.

■

I may have said a few things right
but I have not said everything. I
have this tension. I'd say everything
if I knew what it was. I'd think it is
to get rid of this tension, which seems
to want to snatch up the world unto itself
and reduce it to this: for when I look
onto the street and see a car beautiful
enough to want to own I have forgotten
my tension and the world to me
is one beautiful car after another.

■

Man, I've cooled on anger,
I like living with a bad conscience.
I don't think I could straighten out
a crooked penny. I'd keep it
a souvenir of the time
I wanted it flattened
but suddenly decided
to keep this one moment of wrong.
Since then I feel lively
and different, a little bit
interesting. Shall we say
I'd like to find a crooked buck?

■

IN TRAFFIC

Bird darting across my windshield as I drive,
what are you trying to tell me? Speak up.
I'm entitled to know. How often do you
have to dart past without telling me,
forcing me to guess? Guess what?
Dip your wings in a promise,
but it has happened so fast
I can't be sure.

I can look for good fortune in the next
few days and I can also look for signs
of misfortune, to guard myself against
further encroachment on my life,
so I'm adequately prepared by you,
my windshield bird, but let me know one day
in which guess I am right. I'll wait
and be cautious all the while.

■

THE ESSENCE OF A LIFE

is in the rumble of a train
coming down the track, its dragon lights
at head and feet.

I step back from the platform edge
and stand against the wall,
a blast of tunnel air sweeping past
cool and damp.

The train stops at my feet
with a grinding halt. Its doors
slam open. I get in as if swallowed
and find a seat. With a lurch
and growling, growing speed
the wheels begin to roar.

I am trembling in my seat,
with the steel vibration.
Eyes up and down the aisle
are exchanging apprehension.

Gradually, as the roar persists
without incident, we calm down,
grow bored. Tunnel signal lights
flash by monotonously.
I settle down to wait for my stop.
I'll be glad to get off
so I can make a life
of my own.

■

Joy in the broken bonds of my thinking
is the salvation in my living yet,
as if to bring home to me this fact.

My thoughts are sunk, leaving me to view
my life freely and there it is,
breathing and simple and ordinary
as a shoe which with time
and hard wear will be discarded.

∎

The round, pale globe in the ceiling
is the huge teardrop within me
that I can't release
because inside that teardrop
I lie in a womb
about to be born, mourning
to myself as if it were the life
already I will be living.

I see that where I am
is where I fear being,
but because I do not want
to believe it I lie
in a fetal position,
waiting for another world.

∎

I've wanted to be old and wrung through
so that I could return to my youthful
spirit, without fear of suffering grief
again, having already gone all through
that. I would die young and happy
as the child I was born.

∎

I SURMOUNT

pain at fraud, believing
in my own principle of joy,
that if I would live
as I imagine, each difficulty
must be turned to my employ;
that when I discover its use,
nothing is left
by which I may refuse my joy,
for in my possession is the meaning,
and I am of what each meaning consists,
giving as its reason that myself exists.

■

I uncoil myself and lie straight out
on my bed, with my arms under my head.
I am a floating miracle. If I should speak
it would resound throughout the universe.
I may fly or I may walk. I may lie quietly
or roll over on my side. Whatever I do
I can accomplish all there is to accomplish
and have only to take one small step
and am vanished, yet happy.

This is the meaning I have been dreaming of:
I am happy but do not exist.
I am nowhere to be found,
I am the emptiness that is
and have nothing more to dream,
having reached my dream's goal.
I awaken to take a bath
to enjoy this body and mind.

■

I do not sing for now
but for an eternity of suns
and for the cosmos
of which I am a part
that can sing to it
in that I sing myself,
belong to it
which lives on
so long as there are suns
and these are infinite.

I sing to every sun
that will burn and die
and be replaced. I will
continue singing.

I am the cosmos
at peace with myself
and so it can sing of peace,
of ever becoming,
growing, dying
and being reborn
in the flames
that are the tongues
of my song.

■

 PART IV

SKETCHES

In New York, bus drivers are the only happy men.
They can close doors on people with impunity,
even as it rains, and drive off. Nobody objects,
newspapers set before their faces
in their seats, reading in their spare time
of worse news yet.

In New York, when you say Please,
persons are suspicious that you intend
to rob them or they answer politely
as if to let you know they'd rather
rob you first.

In New York, to enjoy yourself,
you must first beat yourself
on the head with a cop's club.
Reeling over the streets, leer
at the dance hall photos
of girls undressed, for the rent
in a silent room above a flashing neon
that reads Drink Blotto!

■

All right, you have no money, you've given it up
to live the life of a hermit, or worse,
a workingman, a white-collar worker;
still worse, bored from nine to five
with paper and slide rule and hectic cigarette
at a conference table five days a week,
watching and listening and being watched
and listened to.

You can't even let out a good fart
or put a hand slyly up a woman's skirt

at the assembly line, in case you're in
production. Not in a white collar you can't.

So you're doing the worst thing possible
in America, after having given up your wealth.
Are you satisfied? Are others satisfied?

They think they're doing worse than you
and are keeping an eye on you.
They're expecting you to goof off.

They see sometimes on television
or in the headlines who has done a job
of burglary or rape or mishandling funds
or drugs, and right away it's you,
not them, no. It's you.

Next morning they come to work, looking
at the crowd in the subway, and it's you
they're looking for, not themselves.
So how do you like this country,
with everyone on everybody's tail,
like Ring Around the Rosie,
all fall down?

■

HOMELESS

No room of his own,
he crawls into bed
in front of a hundred
pairs of eyes.

No easing of the strain
of living, as one can do

alone, letting the dream
come instead.

■

Poets of The New Yorker
Hotel are very big money,
helps to keep one's balance
in the bank you see people
as clerks, cashiers,
guards, executives have money,
is a problem to others
without money doesn't solve
problems are never finished
with that I leave you
in The New Yorker a sophisticate
usually capable of handling
soils the goods for sale
away with me to South Sea Islands
have been blasted by bomb tests
needed money so I wrote
for The New Yorker Hotel
is a very big time to sleep
and a time to rejoice and a time
to weep for the dead can be found
in cemeteries.

■

The oil burner runs by thermostat,
the refrigerator goes on and off
regularly, the electric clock
never misses accuracy, and when
the washing machine goes on
we have a complete system of production.

Have you looked forward to this,
riding the subway? Can you recall the haste
with which you left your job each night,
sick of this routine? There was the house
to look forward to, where you would receive
love, and so you rode this last sickening
routine of the day to find this source
of pleasure, this comforting release
to be a factory.

How did it happen that all your work and
money could devise only such a place?
You know that in factories you counted
the money earned from them. You concentrated
on that income from the labors in them.
You shaped your thoughts in the image
of factories. When you built your house,
you already had its plan in your thoughts.

■

The vase on the table is never anything
but a vase, though I ask it to turn
into a gull.

For that matter, would a gull turn
into a vase for the wistful person?

I ask you, would you turn yourself
into a clothes hanger for your suit?

Have you been ill lately to want to turn
into another form? Have you dreams
of immortality in which you never die
but turn into another form?

I have envied the cop, the soldier,
the cab driver, the teacher, the lawyer,
the doctor—anyone whose life looks good
to me, as when a cop steps out of his
patrol car to stretch and light his cigarette.
Good job, I say, as I work on my own.
Then he pulls his gun on a poor bastard.
I have nowhere to escape, watching the cop
do his dirty job.

Let's go home, I tell myself after work,
and complain slyly. It will help to hear
the wife herself dream up some new life
for you that you know will turn out
to be a failure right away. Let her talk
and dream. Let it be someone else
for a change, dreaming and making it seem
perfectly normal.

■

The silence of the suburbs is admission
of defeat at living. The lights are on
indoors: the dark is the primeval dark
of the woods, and the cars that speed past
are in a hurry to get through to their homes,
the car lights timidly centered
down the road.

■

It is painful
to look forward
into the emptiness
that will be lacking
all of yesterday
today and tomorrow,

therefore to be lived with
in peace, as all it is.

■

I see a hawk soaring
above the trees, searching
for small birds, singing,
hidden among the leaves.

They too notice
and fall silent,
stir weakly on spindle legs.

The air is clear and calm
in the warm sun, the sky
perfectly blue
without a trace of cloud.
The trees sweep uphill
and then down.

■

Imagine picking up a gun
and after fitting that crow
into your sights you pull
the trigger. He bounces,
to your delight. Contact.
You have the most friendly
feeling; he now knows
you're there. You let him
know and he responded.

■

THE REBEL

When I must look to see where I can run,
then the thing is to run without looking,
to make the break like a frightened animal,
like a child frightened, like a prisoner
who suddenly sees his chance. The mere
motion of leaving protects him,
his captors stunned. Before they can
come to, he is gone.

When you do that, even though
they bring you back to finish your term,
if just to keep on doing it
until you're dead,
you are free.

■

BUT THEN

The rooster crying
as if angry with the light
would prefer
the sun not rise. Cries out
through the dawn but then
resigns himself in silence
in the sun, his work before him,
and his flock awaits.

■

PROPOSITION

Begin with this?
Raise flowers in everybody's heart.

People will bend their heads
to breath in the odor
of their lives: a world
of flower-growers. Then
with heads raised, place flowers
at the hearts of others
to breathe in the odor
of flowers. Am I dreaming?

■

EDITORIAL NOTE

It seems presumptuous to take over the editing of the volume of a poet who had, himself, always been meticulous in his choice and arrangement of poems in each collection. But when ill health overtook David Ignatow and interrupted his assembling and publication of *At My Ease: Uncollected Poems of the Fifties and Sixties,* the poet's daughter Yaedi and the editors at BOA asked me to take over the task of preparing the manuscript. As a friend who has worked closely with the poet over many years, I agreed with trepidation. Aware of the highly personal voice that comprises, and distinguishes, Ignatow's style, I have tried to carry out what I hope would be his wishes in regard to *At My Ease.* The poet had more or less selected and arranged the first section of the book before being unable to continue. The arrangement of the poems in the second section, which he had already chosen, as well as minor editorial changes throughout, are my responsibility. The poems in these pages are some of those that the poet either overlooked as he assembled earlier collections or felt at the time needed further revision.

I have approached the job with humility and offer it to you, assured of your continuing admiration for a poet who, over a lifetime, has produced such a significant body of work.

V. R. T.

∎

ACKNOWLEDGMENTS

The following list of acknowledgments is the most complete possible from information available during the production of this book. We regret any omission, and will include further acknowledgments in a later printing if information is brought to our attention.

"Staying Relaxed" and "They Said" first appeared in *The American Rag*;

"The time comes . . ." in *Anesthesia Review*;

"Love" and "Story" in *Artful Dodge*;

"Subway" in *The Blacksmith*;

"The Daguerreotype" in *A Celebration*;

"Epitaph for a Soldier," "First Generation" and "You spouting about money . . ." in *The Centennial Review*;

"A Fearful Thing," "I Write," and "The Street" in *Chelsea*;

"Separate Windows" in *Exquisite Corpse*;

"A Roman in Manhattan"and "Subway [as the train . . .]" in *The Fun City Observer*;

"Sandis Mountain Range, New Mexico" in *Gulf Coast*;

"Adultery" and "A Rhyme" in *The Hampden-Sydney Poetry Review Anthology*;

"The Question" and "A Song" in *Jewish Frontier*;

"The Promise" in *The Long Islander*;

"Armor" in *Long Island Quarterly*;

"America," "I Listen," "Observed," and "Summary" in *New Myths/MSS*;

"Today" in *The North Shore Review*;

"Sleepless" in *On Good Ground*;

"Questioning" in *Oxford Magazine*;

"Summer" appeared in *Pacific Review*;

"The Saint" in *Painted Bride Quarterly*;

"Careers" in *Panoply*;

"Above and Within," "Credo," and "A Double Grace" in *Pequod*;
"Indignant Lover" in *Poetry Now*;
"Drink" and "Gentle as I try to be . . ." in *Poetry Review*;
"The Executive" in *Red Brick Review*;
"After a Long Walk" in *The Southern California Anthology*;
"Beside the Sea" in *The Tennessee Poetry Journal*;
"Beyond That" and "On the Bowery" in *Underground Rag*;
"The Pen" in *Undine*;
"As They Fly" and "I Will Be Gone" in *Walking Swiftly*, Ally Press;
"For Walt Whitman" appeared in *West Hills Review*;
"This Mystery" and "New Mexico" appeared in *Westigan Review of Poetry*.

■

ABOUT THE AUTHOR

David Ignatow authored seventeen books of poetry. In a career spanning more than fifty years, he received an award from The National Institute of Arts and Letters, "for a lifetime of creative effort," two Guggenheim fellowships, the Bollingen Prize, the Robert Frost Award, and The John Steinbeck Award. Mr. Ignatow was poetry editor of *The Nation* from 1962 to 1963.

Born in 1914, he was raised in Brooklyn, and attended public schools there until 1932 when he entered his father's bookbinding business. He left shortly thereafter to become employed in publicity work. In 1964 he was appointed poet-in-residence at the University of Kentucky, followed by the same appointments at the University of Kansas, Vassar College, and as tenured professor at York College, CUNY. He later taught at Columbia University. He was president of the Poetry Society of America from 1980 to 1984 and poet-in-residence at the Walt Whitman Birthplace Association in 1987, where he served also as a member of its governing board in 1989. He died in 1997.

■

INDEX